DECLUTTERING THERAPY
FINDING FREEDOM FROM CLUTTER
IN YOUR HOME AND MIND

DECLUTTERING THERAPY
FINDING FREEDOM FROM CLUTTER
IN YOUR HOME AND MIND

Katherine Andler

Copyright © 2020 Serpens Publishing
Text copyright © 2020 Katherine Andler

The moral right of the author has been asserted.

All rights reserved worldwide. No part of this book may be reproduced or stored by any means without the express permission of the author. While reasonable care has been taken to ensure the accuracy of the information contained herewith, no responsibility can be accepted for the consequences of any actions based on any opinions, information or advice found in the publication.

ISBN: 9798680015315

DISCLAIMER

The information provided in this book is designed to provide helpful information on the subject discussed. This book is not intended to be used, nor should it be used, to diagnose or treat any emotional or psychological condition. For diagnosis or treatment of any psychological or emotional problem, consult your own family physician or therapist first.

Neither the publisher nor the individual author shall be liable for any specific health needs that may require professional supervision and are not liable for any damages or negative consequences from any treatment, action, application or preparation, to any person reading or following the information in this book. References are provided for informational purposes only and do not constitute endorsement of any websites or other sources. Readers should be aware that the websites listed in this book might change.

Our views and rights are the same: You are responsible for your own choices, actions, and results.

CONTENTS

Introduction..1
Getting Focused by Visualizing a Clutter-Free Home.....5
Resistance to Decluttering...9
When the Past Holds Onto Us, We Hold Onto Stuff...17
A Reason, A Season, A Lifetime....................................23
The Six Box Method...31
The Struggle to Let Go...35
Keeping Things Interesting...43
Digital Clutter..49
Setting Good Maintenance Habits................................55
Looking to the Future..61
Appendix A Hoarding: Further Help............................63
Appendix B Hoarding: Help for Friends and Family....65
Appendix C Smarter Goals...69
Appendix D Clutter Checklists......................................71

Introduction

Our homes are supposed to be havens from the stresses of the outside world. A place we can unwind, rejuvenate and re-energize. But what if our home, or more specifically the stuff inside our home, creates stress? Sharing our personal spaces with lots of junk can have a huge impact on our mental and emotional wellbeing. Clutter often causes us to feel unmotivated, so we avoid getting started on tackling it, and eventually become stuck in the problem.

Our living environments are a reflection of how we feel on the inside. My own journey with clutter began when I was around seven years old (a sure sign that something was amiss in my family of origin). I hoarded all sorts of worthless items underneath my bed, including brochures, often forming strange little attachments to them. Eventually, the things I had collected spilled out beyond my bed, making it difficult for my cold and distant mother to come near me. It was a moat of protection and a source of comfort, though I wasn't to realize this until many years later. Even after I had moved far away from my mother and into my first home, this pattern of living in a chaotic, cluttered environment soon followed me. I once again found myself surrounded by lots of *stuff*.

Not everyone's relationship with clutter will have traumatic family origins, but often the roots can be found somewhere in our early years. We may have been brought up with certain inter-generational beliefs about the value of possessions, have a lack mentality, or we may have grown up with a parent who had a clutter problem.

As an adult with a better understanding of the psychological causes of clutter and hoarding behavior, I watched something familiar playing out in my dad's life. I lost count of the number of times I had cleared and organized his garage for him (an exhausting two to three day job each time), only for the usual mess and disarray to return within months.

It was a lesson in decluttering: you can't go through this process on somebody else's behalf. While there are professionals you can hire that will clear your *stuff* and help you get organized, unless you release yourself from the deeper cause, *stuff* will keep on finding a way back into your life.

For my dad, the frustration of not being able to find anything he needed, when he needed it, eventually forced him to go through the entire contents of his garage, slowly and systematically, over the course of approximately a year. This may seem like a long time, (and if you have dense clutter you should prepare yourself for a lengthy project,) but we shouldn't underestimate the time it takes for us to work through the emotions we've imprinted onto objects. It takes as long as it takes. Decluttering is as much a psychological and emotional process as it is a physical one, and sometimes a slow process is the most effective.

I observed my dad one day at one of his daily twenty-minute appointments with his garage. There was an almost disdain for some of the things he threw away, as though he'd finally realized that most of the items he'd loyally kept hadn't served him one single time. That they had in fact prevented him from finding essential tools he needed, adding time and stress onto the jobs around the house.

The duplicate items he had accumulated were staggering. He had around twenty tape measures 'because he could never find one when he needed it.' So rather than go through the hassle of searching, he would go out and buy another. A short term fix that actually added to the problem of having too much stuff, and made the chances of finding other things less likely. When we've been dealing with clutter for a long time, we learn that searching for some*thing* is a stressful process, rather than simply a matter of going to its usual place and retrieving it. Hoarders and clutterers find a myriad of ways like this to make life easier in the short term and avoid dealing with the root cause.

While there is evidence that clutter and compulsive hoarding runs in families, just because a family member has an issue with clutter (which we may have inherited ourselves,) it doesn't mean it can't be overcome. In these cases, it is an imitated behavioral pattern, supported by the unhelpful beliefs which we may have picked up from the hoarder. Once we have identified those beliefs and the underlying issues, changing our relationship with our *stuff* is much easier. I personally found that as I worked through my mother issues, and changed my mind about the importance of things (which I had learned from my dad) I was able to make more authentic decisions about the things I did and didn't want in my home. Throwing stuff out, even stuff I'd once been extremely attached to, was no longer painful.

Whatever the cause of your situation, and however long it takes to turn it around, let this book be the start of your journey to finding freedom from the clutter in your home and your mind.

Katherine Andler

Getting Focused by Visualizing a Clutter-Free Home

It is likely that you've tried to de-clutter in the past but have either been put off by the sheer size of the job, or the clutter has returned after having gotten rid of it before. Both experiences can be demoralizing and leave you thinking that you'll never be able get rid of the problem. As we will discover, clutter is rarely the problem but rather a symptom, and so we need to prepare ourselves for the possible emotional rollercoaster ahead.

It helps to focus on the benefits you'll reap once you've completed the decluttering process. Maybe not all of the following benefits will be relevant to you, but take a few moments with each and try to visualize how your future home will look and how it will feel to you. You should review these whenever the decluttering process gets challenging and you need to remember why you are doing it.

Household chores will become less stressful and may even be a joy - Clutter makes housework an undesirable chore. People living with lots of junk are unable to clean their home regularly and thoroughly in a way that they would like. A single shelf full of ornaments, paperwork, and other various items will take much longer than is necessary if you have to take everything off in order to just wipe it. And of course all the items will need a dusting and putting back again. Imagine having spaces like this that take thirty seconds or less to clean.

You'll be free to enjoy your space with others – Once you've decluttered, you'll be able to move around your home freely and invite friends and family over. When clutter gets out of hand, we may start to avoid having people over, which is a shame, because we can miss out on connecting with the important people in our lives and the laughter and fun of socializing in our own homes.

You'll experience less stress - Just looking around at clutter is a nausea-inducing sight. Once you free yourself of the things that trigger negative emotions, you'll have items in your home that create positive feelings.

You'll have more money / less debt - When we embark on a decluttering project, an important first step is to reduce the amount of items we are currently bringing into our homes. If we need something such as a tool, and we know we already have it (somewhere), rather than buy a replacement for the one we can't find, we can make a decision to search for it instead. If we do decide to make a purchase, we really need to think carefully so that our home doesn't keep getting refilled. This doesn't have to be a rigid, permanent rule, though these are good habits to form, not only during the decluttering process, but as we maintain this new way of living in the long term. The bonus of course, is that we have more money in our checking accounts. For those of us that have gone into debt because of hoarding, this is a vital resolution until the debt is cleared. Once you are debt-free, decluttering paired with minimalism, will help you to build up savings.

You'll have increased energy - You may have noticed a lot of your energy is spent on your clutter. Whether it is spent moving things so you can use them (laundry off the bed, papers from in front of the TV, books and magazines off the sofa, clothes off the treadmill, etc) or spent searching for something, reassembling it, tripping over it etc, once you have de-cluttered you'll have the energy to spend on the things that are important to you.

A time for new beginnings - After decluttering, many people say it is like starting a new chapter in their life. It is like they have moved into a new home, and they have renewed motivation for making other positive changes in their lives. Get clear about the things you'd like to start doing once your home is in order.

You'll see an improvement in relationships - Clutter can cause conflict within relationships, particularly when one partner is tidy and prefers an organized home, and the other is messy and has too many possessions. Even if it isn't a direct cause of conflict, the disarray around a home can exacerbate marital problems. A cluttered home isn't the best backdrop for solving issues.

Resistance to Decluttering

There are plenty of reasons we might avoid decluttering, despite knowing that our quality of life and peace of mind is being severely impacted by it. If you've ever started but not finished sorting through the piles, or found yourself coming up with excuses, then clearing the resistance to the task is the first step. You'll have a better chance of starting and finishing it if you have complete commitment from the beginning. Reflect on the following reasons and see if any resonate with you:

Fear of regretting a decision - Sometimes we may make a decision to dispose of something and then regret it later. It is a real fear, and if we do it with our stuff, then we probably also do it in other areas of our lives, such as our relationships and careers. Are we somebody that stays in situations that no longer make us happy for fear of regretting making a decision? What is your earliest memory of regretting a change or letting something or someone go? Often this can be the moment that defined how we see decisions and regret.

Most decisions are reversible. If we change career and then later change our mind, we can always return to our original career. It may not be exactly the same job, but this doesn't have to be a bad thing; something obviously wasn't right for you to want to change jobs in the first place. Objects are the same; they can be replaced. The replacement may not be exactly the same; it could be better or just different.

Typically, the real issue is that we think we can't cope with the feeling of regret. But if regret hits, choose to focus instead on the space you've created for the new.

It's too big a job - if we have a lot of stuff, it can be overwhelming to think of the time and energy we will need to spend on it. For dense hoarding, and without outside help, it could potentially be months or, in extreme cases, years of work. One of the best ways to overcome decluttering fear and procrastination is to write a specific plan that breaks down the task, not only by each room, but also by small sections of each room, or even individual piles or collections of items.

You'll be surprised too how much can be achieved with just five or ten minutes per day over a period of time. There is a wonderful quote that is attributed to a number of people, including Bill Gates, that "*most people overestimate what they can do in a day and underestimate what they can do in a year.*" Remembering this can help us to begin that first five-minute appointment with our clutter, and then continue every day until the job is done.

Fear of emotions being triggered - Decluttering can bring on a tidal wave of emotions for us. We may have strong negative emotions attached to our belongings. In fact, it can sometimes be harder to let go of the objects that give us positive emotions. One thing we must remember is that all the time we are surrounded by our things, we are being constantly reminded on a subconscious level, of all the emotions and memories anyway. We are actually living with what we fear, which is why we may be experiencing stress or health issues in the present.

One of the most common emotions that comes up is guilt. We feel guilt for all the things we haven't gotten around to doing, guilt for wanting to let things go, guilt for living the way we have for so long. We can become stuck in this and then it is difficult to move forward with the decluttering. Know that this is something that we can overcome as we go through the pile and process our emotions, rather than waiting for it to pass.

Letting go of familiar comforts - The collection of objects that have been with us a long time can be so hard to let go of, even if its trash. We may fear our life changing and homes looking alien to us when we get rid of all our junk. For some of us, our *stuff* is like a safety blanket, and without it we worry we will feel too exposed.

The decluttering process outlined in this book has no time pressure, so it should not result in any severe or sudden changes, unless of course you're comfortable with this. While it is good to set targets, say to clear a room in one month or to fill a box each day, it is important to go at your own pace. If we view decluttering as therapy, rather than a physical chore, then we will be more willing to pause whenever we need to , to process any feelings that come up. You wouldn't go back to a therapist that raced through a therapy plan and ignored the unexpected emotions that came up along the way. If you want to be rid of clutter forever, you mustn't ignore your feelings now.

Fear of scarcity - Observe any resistance when thinking about letting go of your items as a whole. Sometimes it is due to having a belief that there is a lack of abundance in the world; that if we throw away beautiful or useful things then nothing else will come back into our lives to replace them. This is a belief system that often arises out of growing up without nice things around us, or if we experienced a period of hardship when we couldn't afford such non-essential 'luxuries'. Our formative years can be scarred by comparisons of friends (the haves) and us (the have-nots). Or perhaps we grew up with too much and now fear a fall from grace where we appear to have less to the outside world. We can be forgiven then, when as adults we overcompensate by surrounding ourselves with lots of beautiful, sometimes expensive, non-essential possessions. There is nothing wrong with keeping such items, but our appreciation of them is diminished if we have too many of them, or if we have strong emotional attachments to them for any of the aforementioned reasons.

Take a walk round a large store, visit Walmart or Amazon online, look at all the millions of products that are available, and you'll see that scarcity does not exist.

Fear of loss of identity - The sort of person we once were, think we are now, or want to be in the future, can reflect the sort of stuff we keep. For example, if we like to think of ourselves as being fit and sporty, we may have home gym equipment, a pile of fitness and health magazines, and a large proportion of gym clothes in our closet. These are the things our mind uses to support our identity and prevent us from decluttering, so that we are not exposed as the unfit, unmotivated person we actually are.

Holding onto the illusions of past, present or future self will only hold us back from letting go of our stuff and being our authentic selves. Understandably, we may fear that decluttering will turn us into a completely different person by the end of it. You will still be the same person, but with a different perspective of the material things in your home, and you'll uncover more of your true self. Remember, you are already that person, it is your clutter that is the lie.

What categories of stuff do you have most of? And what part of your identity do they support? Maybe you have lots of tools in the garage because you see yourself as somebody that fixes problems? Maybe your four-sizes-too-small clothes are a big feature in your life because you hope your future self is going to fit into them someday. Or maybe you have lots of books, because you see yourself as an intellectual or even somebody that has the time to read.

Our identity isn't just about the ideas we have about ourselves though. It is also what we think others think of us. Most people at some time in their life have bought and kept stuff to gain validation, acceptance or envy from others. With social media, our insecurities are magnified by influencers and the people we know, most of whom carefully manage their online presence, creating an image of a lifestyle we think we want and need. Clothes, jewelry, art, tech, and cars, are commonly used as status symbols when we feel insecure. Having tons of more general *stuff* is another way we may make ourselves feel safe and successful. However, when we deal with the real issue of insecurity and let go of the need to impress others, we will find freedom in our homes and our minds. This is an incredibly powerful lesson that our *stuff* and decluttering can teach us.

So how many of your items did you buy just for you? And how many were bought to show off or keep up with the Joneses?

When the Past Holds Onto Us, We Hold Onto Stuff

The struggle to let go
Collecting or caching is nothing new. In the animal kingdom, birds and rodents store food for the short and long term. Our early human ancestors also found resourceful ways to make food last. In cold climates they stored meat in ice, and in warmer climates they learned to dry food in the sun. Thankfully, these days we no longer need to collect and store food to survive, but it is easy to fall back on the excuse that collecting is therefore

in our DNA. If this were the case, then every human being would be living amongst dense mountains of *stuff*. While clutter is subjective and on a continuum, not every human being has a constant daily battle with it. Add this to the fact that there is a growing number of humans now following a minimalist lifestyle, who have limited possessions yet are living very comfortably, and you'll understand that clutter doesn't have to have a place in our lives.

The beginnings of a clutter problem

We might not necessarily have begun hoarding in childhood (unless we were an avid collector of something,) but we can usually find the root cause of a developing issue in our formative years.

First, we should examine our family of origin, in particular our parents and our childhood home. Was your childhood home tidy and organized, or was there *stuff* covering every surface? If clutter was familiar to you growing up, then living in an uncluttered space is bound to feel wrong to you in some way. Sometimes the opposite, of not having much, can cause us to hoard in later years as a way of distancing ourselves from what we perceived to be a lack. Fortunately, we can reverse these belief systems and find a healthy balance.

What beliefs did your parents or caregivers have about physical stuff? What was their relationship with the contents of the home? Parents that are attached to items can teach their children that possessions are highly important. Maybe you even felt you were competing with them. What did your parents tell you more directly about *stuff*? That if you broke something then it wouldn't be replaced. That nothing should be wasted. Or maybe they were a bit more blasé about possessions and told you when you lost your favorite cuddly toy they'd replace it. It's our interpretations of our parent's beliefs that can shape our own relationship with material possessions.

Closely linked are the ideas and beliefs our parents had related to money. Did any financial traumas occur when you were growing up, such as a parent losing a job or losing money? A parent with an addiction (which usually requires money,) can leave the family going without essentials or bills not being paid. With our parents already preoccupied, we may not have had anybody to turn to except our *things*, and so this can be where we establish fears about not having enough, or being forced to lose what we already have.

Did you receive inadequate parenting as a result of mental health issues, personality disorders, stress, or parents simply not knowing how to parent? These can all cause children to find solace in their *things*. What do you feel was missing in your childhood? Consider this list and see if anything sticks out:

Love
Sense of belonging
Acceptance
Nurturing

Understanding
Abundance
Security
Safety
Protection
Being important
Being valued
Being seen and heard

As well as our childhoods, we need to examine our life experiences as adults. Many clutter junkies, hoarders and untidy folk, say the onset of accumulating stuff was triggered by a significant, traumatic event in their adult lives. Consider the following:

Divorce or a relationship ending
Death
Children leaving the nest
Moving house
Losing or changing a job
Illness
Abuse
Physical and emotional traumas
Mental health issues

If the issue began in adulthood, then we can probably trace the root cause back to our childhood with any of the previously mentioned issues.

Once we've identified the underlying cause(s) of our clutter, we can use this as a focus as we go through items. For example, if the death of a loved one was the likely trigger, then the emotions that come up during decluttering, such as the inability to let go, are probably residual from that trauma. Clutter can help you grieve and set you free, which may be ironic given the love-hate relationship with may have developed with our *stuff*.

It is incredibly deep work, but if we are to rid ourselves of the physical clutter and not have it return, we need to explore its origins and heal the subconscious issues that are driving it.

Physical objects can't fill an emotional void

People living with clutter or hoarding habits may understand this well, at least on a subconscious level. Our need for whatever it is that we feel we lack: be it love, comfort, safety, security, a sense of belonging, etc, can cause us to seek it out in the wrong places, including in the collecting and storing of objects. Of course, things can't give us what we need, at least not for very long anyway. When the emotional fulfillment that an object gives us is brief and we need to go get more items, it is a clear sign that we are looking to fulfill emotional needs in the wrong place.

At one end of the scale, clutter causes mild to moderate stress and embarrassment, takes away our peace of mind and prevents us from reaching our potential. At the other end of the clutter scale, hoarding is all of the above *and* poses a very serious health and safety risk to occupants and neighbors, it is both the cause and symptom of mental health issues, and it affects our quality of life in more serious ways.

Decluttering as therapy

Like many, we may live with clutter for some time before we finally decide do something about it. When we attempt to get rid of the *stuff* we no longer want, we can come up against a lot of inner resistance without really understanding why. We may give up. Or we may declutter successfully, but soon discover that the junk creeps back in again. Changing the outside is pointless if we don't change the inside as well.

By taking a different approach, by using the decluttering process as therapy, you can heal the underlying issues as you go along. With this method, we can use the clutter to trigger feelings (typically sadness, anxiety, fear, guilt, shame), and then work through those feelings. It is as simple as allowing our minds to bring up the memories, feeling and accepting our emotions, and then learning the lessons about ourselves, other people and the universe. You'll then be free to make authentic decisions about individual items.

A Reason, A Season, A Lifetime

When I observe resistance to letting go of objects, I am reminded of a quote about relationships and friendships, that *"people come into our lives for a reason, a season, or a lifetime."* And that once we know which, we will know exactly what to do. Perhaps we could also apply this to our material possessions during this process.

Reason Objects
Generally, reason objects are practical and serve us in some way, often for a short time period or until we have

learned their lesson. The cardboard boxes you get to declutter your home are a good practical example, as once you have completed this process you'll hopefully get rid of those too!

But it is the items that come into our lives for the purpose of teaching us that have the power to transform us forever. For example, you may have objects that you bought when you were feeling upset, hoping they would make you feel better. The problem when we buy things and we are in a poor frame of mind is that the object can become a constant reminder of the upset, even if it is a subconscious reminder. It is like a souvenir of our unhappy time. Other items may exist in our lives to teach us that *you get what you pay for*, or *everything is temporary*, or *physical objects can't fill an emotional void*.

Look for items you bought because you hoped to start a new hobby. The Learn a Language set, the art materials, the yoga mat...Though you should be honest with yourself about whether you will ever get around to using them, you may have more time and space for them once you have gotten rid of all the other junk.

Season Objects

Most items are seasonal. Even antiquities sitting in temperature controlled museums are disintegrating and have a lifespan, though they will probably last a lot longer than your fair Isle knitted sweater or kitchen can opener. Knowing that items are temporary can be a relief if you're somebody that likes to hold onto things beyond their use and time.

Though an object may no longer be needed or useful to us, it doesn't mean it's not useful to someone else. It is good to remember this when we are struggling to let go of something. We are the custodian of an item in its present form, but an item may have several custodians over its lifetime, and take several different forms. When we talk about different forms, it could be that we find a new use for an item (a plant pot could become an office pen holder for example.) Or an item could be reworked or upcycled (a pair of jeans could be turned into a pair of shorts.) Or an object could be completely transformed through recycling and re-using (such as a laptop that is broken up and the parts used in various other electronic devices.)

There is another reason that most items are seasonal: our tastes are changing and evolving constantly throughout our lives. We don't always notice this, which is why regular decluttering of our homes is essential.

Clothes are a good example of seasonal items, not just because of the fashion industry's own seasonality, but because our tastes, shapes and sizes change, and clothes inevitably wear out. Decluttering our closets can instigate some big changes to our buying habits. If you find you are having to throw out lots of clothes because they are no longer on-trend, you may need to commit to buying less of the latest fashion and more timeless pieces. If you find you're getting rid of lots of clothes because they have worn out, consider buying better quality. They may be more expensive but it is usually more cost efficient in the long run. Or you may realize you don't need to buy as many clothes.

Many of our homewares, such as art and soft furnishings, are often seasonal too. We bring them into our homes because they help pull together the interior style of a room, or simply because we find them beautiful. All too frequently though, these objects become over familiar to us and we stop noticing them. When we no longer see the beauty that already exists in our living spaces, it is easy to understand why we might then want to bring in more of these aesthetic items. Eventually we may realize that we have too many, but when we look at each one individually we see their beauty clearly again, and struggle to let any of them go.

There is a group of seasonal items that are literally 'seasonal'. You might have Christmas decorations stored away, or a tent, or kids paddling pool. These may be items that get used once or a handful of times each year. Keeping them makes sense, but we need to find a proper place to store them.

Lifetime Objects

This is the group of items that we often find the hardest to let go of. If we love them, there is no problem, but sometimes we keep these things out of guilt, family pressure, or some other psychological or emotional bonding. Where there is attachment there is suffering, so even if we decide to keep hold of these things, we may still need to work on letting them go emotionally.

Lifetime *stuff* may include heirlooms and legacy items that have been handed down to us, and anything we have accumulated ourselves that we wish to pass down. Many of these items end up in storage boxes hidden away in the attic, either for their own preservation, because we don't know what to do with them, or we don't actually like them. We may never get them out, and yet it can be almost impossible to try to get rid of them because of the heavy weight of their familial or historical links. Are we being selfish by keeping them, preventing other family members or collectors from enjoying them?

Vacation souvenirs and anniversary commeratives might not have much value, but that doesn't help us when it comes to sorting out which of them to keep and which to discard. We buy such items to evoke positive memories, but having too many of them around us can have the opposite effect. These items become part of our personal history, but you don't need to keep a Venetian mask or Dutch clogs or a Mexican sombrero to remember where you've been, what you have done, who you are or who you once were. Rather than being with us for a lifetime, perhaps the purpose of these objects was to keep the vacation feeling alive for a few months after our return. Many of these items are mass-produced for tourists and are therefore really not that special. The meaning that we add to them makes them special to us.

Sometimes it helps to photograph these items before letting them go, though you probably already have photos of your vacation that evoke stronger feelings anyway.

Any collections you have are probably 'lifetime' too as most people that put the time and effort into curating a collection rarely plan on getting rid of it (because of the time and effort they invested, as well as their passion for the items.) As our tastes and interests change, we may move on to new hobbies without considering that we no longer get any enjoyment out of our past collections.

The factor that all these lifetime objects have in common is that they are items with a story attached to them. If we want to let them go, we need to learn that the story is separate from the object, and we get to keep the story even if we get rid of the item.

It is perfectly possible to go through life without any lifetime objects. An increasing number of people are choosing to lead minimalist lives without such items. It's not necessary to go to that extreme in order to live an uncluttered lifestyle (unless we want to), but it is good to remember that these are usually objects that we don't actually need. If they stop being a positive force in our lives and instead add to our stress, then it is time to reconsider their place in our homes. One question to ask yourself is, (and it is a radical question,) which items would you save in a fire? Usually this helps us to see which items are important to us, and which we merely have an attachment to. Then, to help you make further reductions, could you take a photo of these items and then let them go? Sometimes after decluttering, people find that these 'lifetime' objects are what really matters to them, and they manage to get rid of nearly everything else. This process is all about uncovering what is truly important to us.

When we bring an object into our home, we have no real way of knowing whether it will be with us for a reason, a season, or a lifetime. We may buy something with the intention of it being with us for a while, but then discover this is not to be. Sometimes being able to let go of an item is about accepting that it didn't meet our needs and expectations. Perhaps this is another lesson our *stuff* can teach us; not just about physical objects, but about the limitations of people too.

Problems may also arise when items intended to serve a temporary purpose, or be with us for just a season, overstay their welcome. There should be an easy flow in and out of the home, so we need to develop our ability to let go to ensure things don't get stuck with us longer than they were meant to.

The Six Box Method

There is no one right way to tackle clutter, though plenty of books, articles and videos claim to show us the correct way. I've always found that a six-box method is so simple and straightforward that even a child can follow it, but feel free to change it or try an entirely different method.

For this method you will need six boxes, labeled Keep, Recycle, Donate, Dispose, Sell, and Let Go. You don't have to have all six boxes for the decluttering process. You may, for example, prefer to sell usable items you no longer need rather than donate them to family or charity. You may not need to have a letting go box, as not everyone with a clutter problem has attachments to the junk they have been keeping. And you may be far from a recycling center and have to put everything in the trash. At the very least you will need a Keep box and a Dispose box.

1. Keep box – for items you need and use, that serve you either in a practical way or because they create positive feelings and emotions. Sometimes items need to live in the keep box for a while if they belong in a different room, or you haven't found a place for them yet.
2. Recycle box - check your local recycling center and find out what materials they accept. Some recycling companies can accept items in the mail (such as printer ink cartridges), some may even come to your home and collect. Also consider local organizations that may need items for projects (I found a local craft group on Facebook that turned my old CDs and DVDs into mosaic tiles.)
3. Donate box – this is for the stuff you no longer want but you know could be useful to friends, family, neighbors, and charity.
4. Dispose box - for items you no longer want which are not recyclable or salable.
5. Sell box – for items that you plan to sell at garage and yard sales, or online marketplaces such as Ebay. If you find you are putting lots

of items into here, you may need to set some rules, such as having a lower limit for the profit you are willing to make per item. If it won't make you enough profit it doesn't go in this box.

6. Let Go box – essentially this is for items you don't want to keep, but you don't want to let go of either. They are the things you are attached to that you need a little more time with, perhaps to do some decluttering therapy around, or jut to say goodbye. Sometimes the practice of gratitude for the object is all that is needed. However, if you notice that you're putting the majority of items into this box then you may need to remove it as an option.

These boxes don't have to be big. If you are facing a room that is piled high with *stuff* you might wonder how just six boxes will do, but you should empty them frequently as you go along.

There really isn't anything more complicated to this method than picking up your first object and choosing which box it needs to be put into. Of course, if it was as simple as organizing everything into a few boxes, nobody would have a clutter problem and everybody would have beautiful, tidy living spaces. So as you begin to declutter, the internal work that you will need to do will reveal itself.

The Struggle to Let Go

You may notice when you begin decluttering that you come up with all sorts of reasons for keeping hold of things. Here are the common reasons we often use for keeping an item, and how we can deal with each.

'I might need it one day'
This is such a common reason and one of the main causes of clutter accumulating in our homes. We keep stuff that we don't need and perhaps haven't used for a very long time, just in case we do need it at some point

in the future. But if we did happen to need the item in the future, how easy would it be to get another? Most practical items are replaceable, even items that are a little harder to get hold of can usually be found on the likes of Ebay. By holding on to this item are you preventing someone else who needs it right now from getting use out of it? Also, is this an item someone else has that they could let you borrow if you did need it? Accept the small possibility that you may need to get another in the future, but in the meantime getting rid of the one you have means you can have more space now, and you will be closer to your goal of being free from the junk.

I have bought plenty of items that I've used, and then sold them online, sometimes at a profit. Even if you don't make a profit, you can view any 'loss' as a rental fee, and enjoy the fact that you don't have the item anymore and somebody else is making use of it.

'It might be valuable'

A very common reason for not getting rid of something is the belief that it has value, either right now or at sometime in the future. Quite often, we think an item has more value than it really does, or we expect its future value to be much higher than it actually will be. We need to ask ourselves, 'but does it have value to me and to my life right now?' Keeping an item solely because it has a monetary value prevents someone else getting enjoyment and use out of it.

It is difficult to predict what objects will be collector's items of the future. Even if an object increases in its value, you should be realistic about how much money you will get selling it in ten or twenty years time. There could be lots of people with the same mindset keeping the same items in storage, which will devalue the items you have. You need to think like a businessperson and consider the storage costs, maintenance, and the stress of making sure it doesn't get damaged. Money that is tied up in a physical item is no different from stock sitting in a warehouse. Is it really worth it? Ten or twenty years is a long time to look after an object. If something will have value in the future, then its value today will be relatively higher and people will be willing to pay more money for those potential future profits. Consider selling it now and reap the monetary reward, and the freedom and space from letting it go.

'I will sell it'

This is closely linked to believing that an object has value, though sometimes these items can have little or no monetary value, or they are not worth the hassle of selling. It is our own attachment, and the personal value we mentally imprint onto the object, that makes us believe they will be valuable to somebody else. To you, that cowrie shell is a memento of a once in a lifetime vacation you took to the Maldives where you 'found yourself' in 2009. To everyone else, it's a cowrie shell. Sometimes it helps to have an outside opinion - a friend or a professional organizer - to tell us what is worth selling and what we might be better just giving away. But if you are going to sell something - then sell it. Now. Selling items on the likes of Ebay is another big job on top of sorting out all the clutter. So, as you look at a potential salable object, think about the work involved of photographing it, writing a description, listing it, answering questions from buyers, the packing and shipping. Perhaps you could get other members of the household doing these tasks. If you have a large number of salable items then a yard sale might be a better option, but this too comes with the work of setting it all up and sitting outside your property all day. When we still feel a strong desire to sell something that is probably not going to bring in much money, we need to do much deeper work to uncover and heal the emotional attachment.

Donating salable items rather than selling them, has such a wonderful three-fold effect. Not only will a non-profit like Goodwill benefit from selling the item, but the person who buys it gets to enjoy it too. And you get to be free of it.

'It cost a lot of money'

Sometimes, we know we really need to let go of an object, but we stop ourselves by focusing on the money we spent on it. It might be an item that we've never gotten much use out of, or never really appreciated, but we think only of our hard-earned cash that will be wasted if we say goodbye to it. It is almost as if we feel we are paying for it all over again, when in reality the money is already gone.

It is a fact of life that sometimes we make poor purchase decisions. Rather than thinking of these as a monetary waste, we could instead look for the lessons they bring. Remember back to our Reason, Season and Lifetime objects; perhaps there is a lesson that we need to learn. Maybe we bought an item when we weren't feeling great, and so the object is teaching us not to shop when we are in a low mood. Maybe we were convinced by some glossy advertising campaign that we needed the item in our lives, when actually we are enough without it.

Objects can teach us not to waste more money in the future, and that we don't need possessions to make us feel better or good enough. There are many more lessons that objects can teach us - if we need to learn them. The price of these invaluable lessons has already been paid for when you bought the item. With this in mind you can let go of the items 'that cost a lot of money' with a smile and deep gratitude.

'I will fix it one day'
This is another classic reason our minds use to get us to keep broken junk. The idea that with some gluing, sewing, repainting or replacement parts, we can make an object useful once again. We need to be realistic about the chances of us actually getting around to repairing these items, and our motivation for doing so. How long

have they been lying around waiting to be repaired? Are they worth fixing?

With the increasing concern for the environment and our throwaway society, we certainly need to consider repairing as an alternative to throwing items away, particularly if we plan to replace the old items with new. There are few more satisfying things than spending a weekend fixing or upcycling all the broken things around your home. You don't even need to have special know-how or expertise to fix most items, as there are plenty of from instructional videos and articles online. With the exception of electrical items (which should always be repaired by a professional,) you can gain new skills and check off a whole bunch of things on your to-do list. If this is the route you want to take, then a seventh box called 'Repair' may be needed.

'It might not go to a good home'
This is a real possibility and one we must learn to accept if we are to find freedom from the clutter. Other people might not love and care for the item as much as we did. But when we let go of objects we also let go of the control and responsibility of them. We get to keep the memories and stories attached to the item but the new owner of the item won't see that extra value. They may create their own happy memories around the item and they may end up keeping it for a lifetime. Or it may last a month before it gets broken and thrown out. Focus on your positive memories; that you looked after it while

you had it, and trust that the item will always be out there, in the universe, in some form or another.

Keeping Things Interesting

If you're struggling for motivation you may need to get creative by turning decluttering into a game to keep yourself on track. Here are several ways you can keep decluttering fun and interesting:

Start with five minutes a day. The human mind likes to avoid big tasks. If you have a lot of clutter across your entire home, then start slowly and build momentum. The early stages are usually the hardest until you get into the habit of being decisive and letting things go more easily.

Pick one room to tackle, or play a little game where you declutter one or two things from every room each day. Though completing one room may be more motivating to keep you going on the rest of the house, this can give you a break from the same four walls.

Give away one item each day. This would remove 365 items from your home in one year. If you increased this to two items per day, you would have gotten rid of one hundred and thirty things that you no longer need. You can increase the number of daily items whenever you find it becomes easy. If you own a lot of items that you are very attached to, dealing with one at a time may be more manageable and give you time to say goodbye.

Speed donating. Grab a trash bag and fill it as fast as you can with things you can donate to Goodwill. Fill it, like you've only got twenty minutes to pack for a vacation, with stuff you know you no longer need or have never used. Leave the bag and forget about it for a week. If you don't need anything out of it, then go ahead and donate the bag. The chances are you won't remember or miss any of the stuff that you put in the bag, but if you do, you have given yourself seven days cooling off period. This method can be a good solution if you feel you are lagging behind a schedule, as you can clear a larger number of items from the pile instantly.

Identify the clothes you never wear. Simply hang all your clothes with the hangers in one direction. After wearing an item, face the hook in the opposite direction. After a month or so it will become clear which clothes you use and which you never touch. This will mean your closet decluttering decisions can be taken care of while you focus on the rest of your home.

Create a decluttering checklist. It's a lot easier for your mind to focus on a task when you have a plan for each room. Perhaps there are clothes hanging off the treadmill. Or a pile of mail you haven't gotten around to opening yet. You can then look at this to-do list and choose where to spend your decluttering time. Checking items off on a list is also hugely motivating.

Take the 10-10-10 challenge. Locate ten items to throw away, ten to donate, and ten that need to be put back in their proper place in your home. Not only will this clear out some of the clutter from your home, but also you'll be organizing the things you want to keep.

View your home as a first-time visitor would. It's easy to forget what your home looks like to others. Enter your home as if you're a friend or a buyer and make notes of where all the clutter hotspots are. We aren't just getting rid of clutter; we are creating the home you want to live in.

Take before and after photos. Before you begin decluttering, take photos of every room. You can also hone in on small areas like your kitchen counter, take a picture, and then quickly clear everything out of the area and take an after photo. Once you see how your home could look, it becomes easier to start decluttering more areas.

Enlist the help of a non-judgmental friend who lives an uncluttered life. Have a friend or family member go through your home, and ask them to suggest a handful of contents you could get rid of. A friend can be helpful if you are having trouble letting go of things. Your friend can listen to your reasons for keeping the items and offer an outsiders point of view. A word of warning though; sometimes bringing in people that we know can really test friendships!

Pick any room in your home and go through every single item, placing each one into one of the six boxes. Don't skip a single thing, if you pick something up then you have to process it. If you can't decide which of the boxes to put it in, you don't get to move on until you do. This may take days, weeks, or months, but stick with it and eventually you will have cleared the room of junk. Sometimes we just have to be firm with ourselves.

Play the clutter lotto. If you don't know where to start, let chance, or the universe, make the decision. Put numbered stickers on items, piles or boxes, and then draw the numbers from a hat. Seeing the numbers and the clutter diminish can be extremely satisfying.

Digital Clutter

Years ago non-physical clutter didn't even exist. But now so much of our lives is online or digitized that this area has become a major source of mess and stress for many of us. If you have a clutter problem in your home, then you probably have a digital clutter problem too.

Thanks to technology, there are now tons more places to store junk documents, mail, photographs, videos, unwatched TV show recording etc. And because all this information doesn't take up much space (or none at all if we use cloud storage,) we can happily ignore it. Except when we need to dig out that important document from hundreds of unnamed files, or find a particular photo from a shared memory that has just come up in conversation. Or find that the device is unbelievably slow because the memory is nearly full. In these moments, we discover that the stress from digital stuff is no different to living in a house full of physical stuff. We've only moved it to a place where we can forget about it more easily.

Here is a checklist to help you get started on organizing your digital life:

Emails
    Delete old Emails
    Unsubscribe to and block unwanted emails
    Set up automation rules to organize your email account and prevent further junk flooding your inbox
    If the spam problem is bad, consider a second email account - one that you reserve for important emails only. Your other email address can be given out when you sign up to websites etc.

Computer, storage devices and cloud storage
    Go through every file and document
    Delete old downloads
    Organize folders
    Sort homescreen shortcuts

Cellphones, tablets and other devices
    Remove the apps you don't use
    Delete old contacts
    Delete old messages
    Delete old voicemails
    Switch off unimportant notifications
    Go through photos (see below) and videos
    Go through your downloads and files
    Delete music you no longer listen to
    Delete downloaded podcasts

Social media
    Unsubscribe to blogs and social media accounts that don't enrich your life
    Delete social media accounts that you don't use or you find are a drain on your time

TV Recordings
    Delete recordings you have already watched and don't want to watch again
    Be realistic about how much time you have to invest in new TV shows you haven't watched yet (these can be just like broken objects, mocking you for yet another thing you haven't gotten around to doing)

Photos

Before smartphones and digital cameras came along, taking ten shots of the same thing would be an expensive folly for an amateur photographer, not to mention it would take up almost half the exposures on a roll of film. Today. we don't need to worry about the expense of getting bad photos developed, and the number of photos we can take is only limited by the size of the memory card. Perhaps this is where most of the problem lies; we can now take and store thousands of photos on a small card or cloud drive, so we don't have much of an incentive for organizing them. But a cluttered photo collection - whether physical or digital - is not an appealing place to visit, so often these photos don't ever get looked at again. Their existence however, can still be a huge source of stress.

Duplicates and almost duplicates. Pick the photo that captures the emotions and moment well and discard the rest or pass them to others.

Photos you don't actually like. We all have photos we don't like due to bad lighting, bad angles, bad hair...the list goes on. If there are other people in the shot you want to keep, crop the photo. But don't keep photos that don't bring you joy.

Photos with people you don't know or don't like.
These may include people from your past relationships or friendships, random shots of wildlife, or your boss at the office party.

Technically bad photos. Any blurry, grainy, underexposed, overexposed, weird-angled, unidentifiable images can go.

Setting Good Maintenance Habits

Maintaining a clutter-free lifestyle is dependent on two things:
    1. Controlling the stuff coming into the home
    2. Regularly clearing out and organizing the stuff we currently have

Fortunately, maintenance is a dream compared to the hard work of decluttering, particularly if you are now in the habit of letting things go and getting organized.

During the decluttering process we need to manage what is coming into the home. (There is no point getting rid of the old stuff if there is new stuff coming in, especially if it is at a greater rate.) But once we are on top of the junk, we can go ahead with some of the purchases we've been putting off.

However, we need to be aware of how much *stuff* is coming into our home, regularly review our buying habits (particularly if shopping was the cause of the clutter,) and identify the areas that tend to get disorganized. Are we buying too many new clothes, is mail stacking up in a pile on the kitchen counter, are Amazon shipments arriving daily? If we live with others, we won't be able to control everything that comes into the home, but if we know the sources we will know where we need to focus our regular decluttering and re-organizing.

The Closet
Clear closets once a season or once a year, depending on how often you buy new clothes, and whether you have kids that are growing out of clothes quickly. Be ruthless with clothes that don't fit, haven't been worn, are worn out or damaged, or are out of fashion.

If you are finding that you are throwing out a lot of clothing perhaps consider changing your buying habits.

Accessories and shoes can get really disorganized, so some well-labeled storage boxes may be what is needed here.

Mail

If it seems like every flat surface in your home serves as a landing zone for mail, now is the time to adopt a new strategy. Get into the habit of sorting the mail immediately each day. Junk mail can be so time consuming and one of the main reasons we may avoid dealing with the mail properly. Look into services that you can sign up to that stops marketing communications and catalogs, or get in touch with the companies and cancel them directly.

Be sure to place invoices in a designated place to remind you to pay them, then, once paid, discard the payment notice or file it away.

Make sorting the mail more appealing by doing it in an area where there is a paper-basket and shredder nearby.

The Entrance

Everyone makes the porch and entrance hallway their dumping ground. A place to abandon workday attire. Backpacks, lunch boxes, briefcases, gym bags, keys and, of course, shoes! So many shoes. The key to keeping this space organized is to utilize storage and clever organizers. Use a shoe rack or a low shelf with compartments so that everyone can store their footwear, install hooks for coats and storage bags. Get kids into the habit of putting shoes and bags into their proper place when they come home from school. Set the example here, don't we all like to kick off our shoes and shed our work gear at the door? But it takes less than a half-minute from everyone to keep this space tidy and welcoming.

Office

The office all too often becomes the junk room of the house. Even if we don't use it as an office full time, it offers a quiet workspace whenever we need it - providing we keep it tidy and organized. Ideally, there should be some sort of system for important documents. Consider organizing these into files such as receipts, car, home, savings and investments, insurance, tax etc, and then you'll be able to find whatever you need, quickly, and without having to go through the entire contents of the office each time. If you have documents and receipts that you need to keep for a certain number of years for tax purposes, create a folder with the date you can destroy them.

We often underestimate how long it will take to organize paperwork. Unlike a lot of the other stuff in our homes, we need to read through papers carefully before deciding whether it is a keep, trash or shred item. Separate documents should be sorted and archived regularly - make an appointment with yourself once a week, once a month, or even daily if you get a lot of paperwork. Install a mail basket to sort unread mail and keep only the supplies you need such as pencils, paper, and a booklet maker on hand. Everything else can be stored in a drawer or on a shelf and put away again after each use.

Bathroom

Despite being one of the most frequented rooms, the organization of the bathroom usually leaves something to be desired. Every six or twelve months, take a garbage bag and throw away expired cosmetics or medicines and anything else you come across, such as a most-empty shampoo bottles. Most toiletries expire in twelve or eighteen months, so this way you'll keep on top of the out of date items. The medicine cabinet will require close attention.

Install containers (if you have the space,) to store items such as cosmetics, elastics, hairpins, brushes, etc. Consider providing everyone with a shower accessory tray so that everyone's stuff is kept organized (and fights over shampoo are minimized).

The Family Room

It is impossible to relax in the family room if it is crowded. Keep your coffee table free from homework, mail and magazines by using a storage system or keeping those things out of the space. Designate a place for electronic devices, such as the TV remote control, so you never have to look for them again. Make it everybody's responsibility to keep this room tidy. Regularly throw out old magazines, old toys, and anything else that is no longer used.

The family room can get very messy, especially if we have young kids. Clever storage solutions are vital - we may walk in and find every single toy is out on the floor, but we won't be as stressed if we know that every one of the toys has a place and can be tidied away.

The Refrigerator
Have a weekly clean-out of the refrigerator to get rid of old leftovers, the almost empty salsa pots, or anything that hasn't been used in six months, open or not. If you do this before you go grocery shopping you'll have a better idea of what you've run out of and what you still have left, so you'll be less likely to over-buy.

Don't forget the freezer. Anything that has been in there for more than nine months should be thrown away. The same should apply to your pantry and food cupboards.

The 'Junk Room'
Don't ignore the places we commonly refer to as junk rooms, such as the attic, garage, spare room, office, and under stair closets. We may use these to store long-term junk and trash that we like to forget about when we close the door, but even if you are storing contents in these rooms long term, there still needs to be order, and everything need to have its place.

Looking to the Future

Don't get disheartened if clutter tries to put in a reappearance, either in a small or big way. When we've lived with *stuff* for a long time, it can take a while to adjust to the new lifestyle. We've been through some big changes. New clutter is either here to test us, or a sign that there is more inner work left to do.

Through this process you have probably learned that life is all about change. Maybe the reason we used to hold onto so much stuff was to create stability in this crazy and ever-changing world. But we now know that we can find more stability and peace in a home that is clear of stuff that doesn't serve us.

You may also have noticed that the more items you get rid of, the easier decluttering becomes. At some point you might have started to enjoy it, or even love it. When a shift like this happens, when we have developed the skill of letting go and accepting change, it becomes less likely that we can ever go back to living in a cluttered home.

When the decluttering is complete and you're into the maintenance routines, you'll find you have more energy, less stress, and a renewed motivation for life. You'll now have the space in your home to workout, meditate, bake, and watch television without a mountain of stuff framing the TV set. You'll be able to concentrate more easily, so dreams like starting a business or writing a book can become a reality. Perhaps while decluttering you found that art set you bought twenty years ago. Now is the time to start new projects or take up new hobbies. Your home and its former contents are no longer distracting and holding you back, but supporting you in the life you want.

You have one final task: to get rid of those six boxes.

Appendix A
Hoarding: Further Help

Most of what we've discussed concerns clutter and mild to moderate hoarding. There are actually five levels to hoarding, and at the extreme end of the scale the clutter is dense, exits are blocked, rooms are no longer usable as they were intended, and there may be dead rodents... We've all seen Hoarders on TV. When the situation gets to these levels, it is much harder to overcome the problem with just the advice given in this book. Though the emotional causes and solutions remain the same, getting rid of the physical hoard may require more than six boxes and a bit of motivation. In most cases, the homeowner has a compulsive disorder that would benefit greatly from professional support. Organizers who specialize in excessive clutter clean-ups and hoarding may be in the right place to offer some of this help. After all, they have seen everything and heard all the reasons that have caused their clients to become hoarders. They may be able to recommend hoarding support groups, counselors, therapists, or if necessary, psychiatrists, to work on the OCD (Obsessive Compulsive Disorder) and other aspects of the problem. We don't have to go through this process alone.

Appendix B
Hoarding: Help for Friends and Family

Denial can be a big feature of excessive clutter and hoarding behavior, which makes it difficult for sufferers to reach out and seek the help they need. It is therefore their loved ones that often realize there is a problem first. Shame is also a strong feature of hoarding. Friends and family, who, having been prevented from visiting for years, are usually shocked at the extent of the problem.

Bringing up the matter can sometimes result in conflict if the sufferer isn't ready to hear it. It is best to broach the subject gently, without judgment, and take it from there. Remember people can only be helped if they want to be. If they aren't ready, and you put pressure on them to clear the hoard, the problem will still remain and the *stuff* is likely to return. It is the behavior that is the problem, not the *stuff*.

This can be particularly difficult for partners and family members (especially if they are tidy, minimalist and organized types) to accept. Many relationships have broken down over clutter. And of course being surrounded by mountains of mess is not conducive to dealing with relationship issues in a positive way.

There are of course situations that demand intervention from health and adult services. This can be a dilemma for loved ones, but when children are involved or the home is a safety hazard, it really is a no-brainer. This may be the wake up call the sufferer needs to get help and make the necessary inner changes, so you can make the call without guilt.

Support groups for hoarders usually also offer support to the partners, family and friends of hoarders. The information and help you can get from these organizations can be invaluable, and you can learn a lot from recovering hoarders.

Living with a hoarder is exhausting. It's not just being surrounded by mountains of stuff that drains us, but the inner mind of the hoarder can be chaotic, compulsive, depressive, anxious, and even disturbed, depending on which emotional and mental issues are present. Our own self-care is vital.

Remember, nobody has to live in a home that makes them feel stressed, uncomfortable, embarrassed, or ill. And certainly nobody has to put up with any aggressive, manipulative behavior from the hoarder, simply for suggesting they might need to get rid of a few things.

Sadly, many people endure these situations. This is why codependency support groups are also recommended for those living with a hoarder. While we may protest on a daily basis about the mess, by remaining in that situation, we are at the same time telling them that it is ok. Actions speak louder than words; we are enabling the hoarder. We need to learn to say no. We need to know that we can still be supportive and loyal to the person, even when we are living in a clean, uncluttered home somewhere else.

Appendix C
Smarter Goals

Setting SMARTER goals before we declutter can be a great way to stay focused, and you can use this for both the big goal of decluttering the whole home, and smaller goals such as sorting a small pile or drawer. It helps if we write the goals down, but you don't have to; you can use them as pointers to reflect upon before setting to work.

Goals should be:

Specific – such as 'to gather and sort all the magazines into one pile.'

Measurable - E.g., to reduce a pile by 60%

Achievable – setting an achievable goal is about knowing what you are capable of. You may be raring to press ahead and get it all done now, but can the clutter really be dealt with all in one go?

Relevant – how will this help your bigger goal of decluttering your whole home?

Time bound – how long will you give yourself to complete the goal?

Evaluate - though it is always nice to have someone give us positive feedback, it is more important that we give ourselves positive feedback for the work we have completed. So always take a moment out to admire the effort you have put in.

Reward – if you used to reward yourself by buying things, you may need to change this habit. But there are many ways to reward yourself for completing a decluttering goal, such as taking a long bath and reading a book, or going for a walk.

Appendix D
Clutter Checklists

Clutter checklists are a way of keeping track of the decluttering process and the regular maintenance you'll need to do. The following lists are to help get you started, but you can create your own checklists that are specific to your home and needs. You could, for example, give each person in the household their own checklist with a list of decluttering chores to do.

Many parents who have had an issue with clutter worry they may pass it on to their children, but giving children clear to-do lists that they can check off teaches them there is satisfaction in decluttering, and gives them a taste of responsibility in running the household.

KITCHEN
- ☐ Refrigerator
- ☐ Freezer
- ☐ Pantry / food storage
- ☐ Kitchen counters
- ☐ Cabinets
- ☐ Drawers
- ☐ Under the sink
- ☐ Kitchen appliances
- ☐
- ☐
- ☐
- ☐
- ☐
- ☐
- ☐

BATHROOM

- [ ] Bathroom counters
- [ ] Cabinets
- [ ] Drawers
- [ ] Toiletries
- [ ] Shower/bath
- [ ] Medicine cabinet
- [ ] Towels and wash cloths
- [ ]
- [ ]
- [ ]
- [ ]
- [ ]
- [ ]
- [ ]

BEDROOMS

☐ Under bed
☐ Bedside tables / cabinets
☐ Closets
☐ Linens and sheets
☐
☐
☐
☐
☐
☐
☐

CLOSETS
- [ ] Shoes
- [ ] Sort clothes
- [ ] Accessories
- [ ]
- [ ]
- [ ]
- [ ]
- [ ]
- [ ]
- [ ]

LAUNDRY ROOM

☐ Clean counters
☐ Fold laundry
☐ Laundry products
☐
☐
☐
☐
☐
☐
☐

LIVING ROOM / FAMILY ROOM

☐ Sort magazines
☐ Books
☐ Toys
☐
☐
☐
☐
☐
☐
☐

OFFICE

☐ Files
☐ In and out tray
☐ Sort mail
☐ Paperwork
☐ Empty shredder and waste paper basket
☐
☐
☐
☐
☐
☐
☐

MISCELLANEOUS

☐ Clean out wallets, purses, briefcases etc
☐ Car
☐ Outside areas e.g. garbage, outside storage
☐
☐
☐
☐
☐
☐
☐

REFERENCES AND REOURCES

The Institute for Challenging Disorganization has resources such as fact sheets. The Clutter-Hoarding scale is widely used to assess the health and safety of a home and the scale of the problem.
challengingdisorganization.org

The National Association of Productivity and Organizing Professionals has information on how to hire a professional and a directory of professionals that can help with clutter control, chronic disorganization, digital clutter, hoarding behaviors, and general home organizing.
napo.net

Clutterers Anonymous is a 12-step fellowship recovery program for hoarders
clutterersanonymous.org

ALSO BY KATHERINE ANDLER

Self-Guided EMDR Therapy & Workbook: Healing from Anxiety, Anger, Stress, Depression, PTSD & Emotional Trauma

Self-Administered EMDR Therapy: Freedom from Anxiety, Anger and Depression

Self-Administered EMDR Therapy: Freedom from PTSD and Emotional Trauma

Self-Administered EMDR Therapy: Overcoming the Effects of Bullying

Freedom from Maladaptive Daydreaming: Self-Help Strategies for Excessive and Compulsive Fantasizing

Printed in Great Britain
by Amazon